The Mai Today

Jan Swartz

Illustrated by Triska Seeger

DOMINIE PRESS
Pearson Learning Group

ISBN 1-56270-271-8

Printed in Singapore
4 5 6 7 8 9   07 06 05

Dominie
Press
Pearson Learning Group

1-800-321-3106
www.pearsonlearning.com

The mail came today.

Mom got a letter.

Dad got a letter.

My sister got a letter.

And I got a big box.

Is it a truck?

Is it a book?

No, it's a ball.